WINTER.

WINTER.

Zoe McGarrick

Copyright © 2025 by Zoe McGarrick
All rights reserved. No part of this book may be reproduced in any manner whatsoever without written permission except in the case of brief quotations embodied in critical articles and reviews.
First Printing, 2025

Thank you to my friends, especially Lydia because this is hers too.

Contents

Dedication		iv
1	COLD	1
2	THE WOLF	3
3	ROSE	4
4	HANSEL AND GRETEL	5
5	ASH	7
6	A DANGEROUS STORM	8
7	SPARK	10
8	SLEEP	11
9	RED	13
10	TURN	15
11	SNOW WHITE	16
12	THE WINTER GHOSTS	17
13	FIRST KISS	18
14	A ROOM OF ONE'S SKIN	19
15	TO LIVE IN HELL	20
16	WHEN LIFE TOOK DEATH	21
17	THE END	23

About The Author   24
About The Artist   25

1

COLD

Walls crawl from snow like vines in ancient temples,
    Gilded windows from ice like mist on a lake,
Breath curls into a bed like a newborn,
Beating a heart against Winter,
Almost falling apart, veins clinging cement.
The house groans and shakes in the wind
And whispers in the moonlight, dimmed.
Ice can crawl in eyes like maggots into a corpse,
Slowly slitting veins of blue iris like the bite of a viper's look;

Feeding a pain that fades over time like the numb touch of a ghost,
    Surrounding a family of snowmen and ice queens
    Blind to what lurks in the shadows of what their house seems.
    The season stains the houses red like honesty in heart,
    Inside lurks a lacing of blue in each eye like the tying of a noose,
    From a frozen home that caters to the cold and numb,
    A heat burnt out by the ice in blood like ink in water
    Christmas can be where the numb are led to slaughter.

2

THE WOLF

Howling, the night's ink thickens,
    A blanket over nature;
Smothering its short breath
As the wolf wakes for death.

The trees whisper amongst themselves,
Hidden in the shadows,
Their breath quick and short
As the wolf rustles their dead children his paws have caught.

Prowling, hungry for flesh,
Greedy for blood,
The moon; a lighthouse to chaperone
The wolf's desires from nature's throne.

Branches groan, forced to witness
An innocent wander:
Red stains her ready
For the wolf is hungry.

3

ROSE

Thorns that bruise aren't thorns at all.
    The roses that wilt weren't strong for us all.
The stems bend for light when darkness is near.
But what warrior would find that sincere?
The single rose that blooms
Will have its beauty assumed
As strength in place of bravery
But roses of this kind are bound in slavery.

4

HANSEL AND GRETEL

B rother and sister left by the Winter
To suffer the cold in silence.
Their mother knew that tax was a hunter,
Their father cared but kept up the alliance,
To leave the children behind, scared.

Hansel and Gretel, two children, too young.
They grew up by the wolf pit, taking what they flung
As they survived by each other's side
And grew to love and confide.

A boy and a girl found in the Summer.

Bodies white as snow,
Fingers blue and now eyes to hold a glimmer.
The lovers died in the Winter,
Holding onto each other,
Naked and fragile as a statue,
Their last words had been "I love you."

5

ASH

My Father is a scared man
who ties golden embers into grass, and conjures
up in ashes, a magic
trick, a marvel.
Destruction in a simple flicker.
The world, breathes,
the grass waits,
and now the air is thicker.

6

A DANGEROUS STORM

Lightning strikes in a blink of an eye,
    Delicate blue veins trapping the clouds,
Safely locked in midnight.

The ground shakes in anger at hesitation
So prominently subtle, a groan quakes
And quirks the lips of the stars.

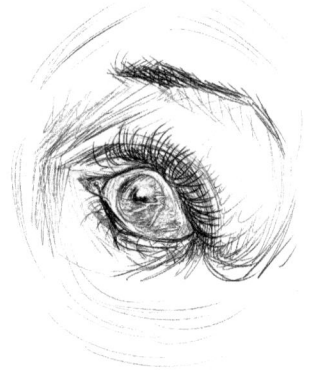

Burning before us, waiting to explode;
Nature's own fireworks and the
Mind scorches in flashes of memory.

Or dreams of darkness and some light
Or reflections of light brought out by darkness.
A dangerous storm must die down in here.

7

SPARK

Lightning struck my chest,
    A spark traced my lips,
Your bright blue eyes flashed,
Hands fogging my mind.
The storm that swells inside
Is what I cling to.

Heartbeat thundering,
Nails biting smooth skin,
Your whisper tickles
My soul and desire.

My eyes speak sonnets,
My body watches,
Lips inspire a flame.
The spark you nurture.

8

SLEEP

Drift into a deep darkness,
    Where warmth is no longer a stranger.

Let your body rest
Where dreams no longer hinder.

Closed, the mind's cage is open,
You are free, you are wild.

No idea opposed, sleep takes you again
To a dream to leave you beguiled.

Let the light fade,
Open your soul,

No one can hurt you in the shade,
Not even the villain Cold.

9

RED

In the midnight moon glow
  The red cape is soaked in blood.
The little girl is all for show
When the real beast is caked in mud.

She howls and squirms in the day,
Waits for the night to come
So she can snarl and scratch away
When the real beast makes her dumb.

The trees shade her torn body,
Bruises scatter the black skin
Of a nobody and a somebody
When the real beast recovers her sin.

She claws the dirt
and scatters the bones
Blood clings to her skirt
When the real beast creaks and moans.

The moon is full and smiling
Watching as the little girl changes
Her skin and bones writhing
When the real beast reveals her as strange.

Fur covers the cut skin of the girl
Her teeth and sharp and ready to kill
All that evil brings begins to unfurl
When the beast is ready to kill.

10

TURN

You kissed my soul with infested tongues,
    Venom sunk down before I could reach you
Now breathing in my own air
Too much with flooded lungs
That don't know if this could reach you.

The poison spit in my eyes;
I can't help but see
You're a lie of a lie
And the shadow of a shell that can't even keep you

My fists hitting the glass,
Snakes hidden around rose stained ankles
Tightening flames that lick past
the luck of the draw is just a sample
if the dark rejected you I must come at last

11

SNOW WHITE

Glistening blood drops from the rose
    That collects earth's nectar
And watches where the crimson goes
In the absence of a protector.

Soft snow blinds the eye
White as gold
As precious as a lie,
The land stands bold.

The crow circles above
Black and callous
Enemy to the dove
And the heart of the jealous.

12

THE WINTER GHOSTS

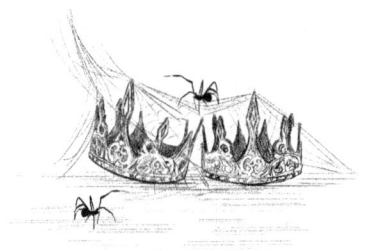

I n deepest snow laced silks,
    A royal crest in silver sits,
  Prized beyond all that grow,
  Heavy lump under snow.
  Ice scraped and scratches
  Old, dead Latin-lost,
  Tell the white-haired witches come,
  And the new with nature ghosts belong.

13

FIRST KISS

Cold brick tickles your skin,
My fingers dance on your palms,
Waiting for something to begin.
The rush of silence has its charms
When we let it dance between skin and the light
Lights up a laugh in the throat
My lips are addicted to
Printing permanence like a photograph,
Pixels struck by the sweet moans from you.

14

A ROOM OF ONE'S SKIN

In her lips laced meanings,
    Liquid euphoria; a breathe;
Pushing through-chest
To burst and room in
Another skin. - Where skin Becomes a whisperer; it's
A ghost touching it's tombstone:
A semblance of home,
Teeth turn to grin, hands
Our skeleton, sacred and scarred
Entwined in a moment of an hour:
Of a life of a door
Opened by just a kiss.

15

TO LIVE IN HELL

To burn would be beautiful
    Placed a-top the Earth
Like a hiker onto a bear trap.
The ground wounded in mirth,
Our eyes swim with dreams,
Of beauty, of promise, of faith,
of a life more than it seems,
where to be in Hell is to go
to Heaven,
And there may you rest,
After passing in all the Seven.

16

WHEN LIFE TOOK DEATH

Death held out that skeletal hand;
    Bone cloaked in shadowy black,
So dark the eyes struggled to land
On the body the being lacked.

Death paused, mist filling the hills,
Green dispersed into grey,
The skin faded, absorbed by Winter chills,
As midnight took over from day.

Death's dark eyes seemed bright
With Death grasping the person so young,
The answer didn't seem oddly right.
But the answer of "no" caught on the tongue,

Life watched it over with ache in heart,
The glowing eyes and skin blurred in midnight,
As they asked for them not to part,

When they had so much future left in sight.

Life knew the cruelty of Death,
But also, the strict rules darkness obeys,
But what is the body without its breath,
What is the sun without its days.

Life, like the moon in the jet-black sky,
Waited as Death stopped,
Dark eyes shifted onto the one who had to die,
And let Life be the one he adopts.

The person stared, oddly hesitant,
Pain in their eyes and now calm,
The first breath of relief was evident
That Life had done the most harm.

17

THE END

G old encrusted voice
　　Sing to me my Six
Where shadows crawl
Oddly warm
Let me find my home.

Zoe McGarrick has written short stories and poetry. She published a novel, *The Painter's Wife*, in 2022 and a poetry collection, *Winter.* in 2024. She has been featured in Bananamilk Magazines' Biblioteca Anthology (2024), and Word Tonic's Food for Thought (2024), and Mugwort Magazine (2025). They are a horror and gothic fiction fanatic, inspired by Shirley Jackson and Angela Carter, who highlight women's history and struggles through her work.

As well as writing, Zoe is also an artist, with her most recent painting being showcased in Girlpane's inaugural exhibition this year (2024). She currently resides in Oxford, United Kingdom, and is always working on the next project, with a horror zine set around Oxford, and another novel on the way. Zoe's work often evokes an eerie atmosphere of dread, mystery, and plays with language inspired by gothic works before her.

About The Artist

Illustrations and cover artwork by Lydia Swallow.

Lydia Swallow is an artist based in Devon, with a Bachelor of Arts in Animation Production and a Master's in Film Editing. She works with various authors and companies, producing animations, illustrations, and editing advertising videos that blend creativity with precision. Lydia's work, characterised by influences, often features glowing, mystical elements that evoke a sense of wonder and intrigue.

Follow for more of Lydia's artwork and updates on Instagram @lydiaswallow_ and at her website: lydiaswallow.squarespace.com

For business inquiries: lydiaswallow7@gmail.com

www.ingramcontent.com/pod-product-compliance
Lightning Source LLC
Chambersburg PA
CBHW052207070526
44585CB00017B/2112